W9-AUJ-448

An Important Message to Our Readers

This book provides information and general advice about the law. But laws and procedures change frequently, and they can be interpreted differently by different people. For specific advice geared to your specific situation, consult an expert. No book, software or other published material is a substitute for personalized advice from a knowledgeable lawyer licensed to practice law in your state.

The information in this book is provided "as is" without any warranty of any kind, either expressed, implied, or statutory, including, but not limited to, any warranty that this information will conform to any specifications, any implied warranties of merchantability, fitness for a particular purpose, or any warranty that the information will be error free.

In no event shall the author or publisher, or the author's or publisher's contractors or subcontractors, be liable for any damages, including, but not limited to, direct, indirect, special or consequential damages, arising out of, resulting from, or in any way connected with this book, whether or not based upon warranty, contract, tort, or otherwise, and whether or not loss was sustained from, or arose out of the results of, or use of, the information contained in this book.

3rd Edition

Patent Searching Made Easy

How to Do Patent Searches on the Internet and in the Library

by David Hitchcock

This book was last revised in: November 2005.

Third Edition

Front Cover Photo   NASA

Back Cover Photo   NASA

Hitchcock, David, 1956-
    Patent Searching Made Easy / by David Hitchcock.—3rd ed.
    ISBN 1-4116-5838-8

Dedication

This book is dedicated to my wife Sylvia, who was always there when it mattered and to Jennifer, for putting up with a daddy who was constantly working in his office.

Acknowledgements

All screen shots from the USPTO website are courtesy of the United States Patent and Trademark Office. All screen shots from the EPO website are courtesy of the European Patent Office. All screen shots from the Defense Technical Information Center are courtesy of DTIC.

The author also gratefully acknowledges and thanks the Thomas Register, Google, Medical Informatics Engineering and the Microsoft Corporation for granting permission to use various screen shots in this book.

About the Author

David Hitchcock has degrees in physics and engineering, and has worked as a computer consultant on such diverse projects as the MX missile, the Milstar satellite program and advanced capability torpedoes. He has focused on patent searching and new technology for a number of years. Author of a training video on patent searching over the Internet, Mr. Hitchcock has also given presentations on the subject to inventor groups.

Table of Contents

Introduction

Part 1: The Basics

1. Introduction to Patents and Patent Searching   1

2. Tools and Resources   17

Part 2: Internet-Based Patent Searching 23

3. Patent Searching at the PTO Website 25

4. Advanced Patent Searching at the PTO Website 53

Appendices

A. Patent and Trademark Depository Libraries

B. Forms
Classification Search Sheet
Class Finder Tool

C. Summary of Searcher's Secrets

Glossary

Preface

This third edition of *Patent Searching Made Easy* has been completely updated to include the latest changes at the PTO's patent searching website and the latest resources available at the Patent and Trademark Depository Library system. A chapter covering the European Patent Office has also been added.

It is my sincerest hope that you find this guide informative, easy to use and helpful in your invention development efforts.

David Hitchcock
November 2005

Introduction

If you are an inventor or owner of a business engaged in research and development, this book shows you how to:

- quickly "check out" any new idea, to see if anyone else has already patented it

- verify the patent status of ideas submitted to you for development (if you are a potential developer)

- save lots of money in legal fees, and

- avoid reinventing the wheel.

A. Check out New Ideas

You come up with what seems like a new way to solve a problem or accomplish a task. But you wonder if somebody has already trod this ground before you, and either succeeded in obtaining a patent or proved that your idea is not feasible?

You have been told that to answer these questions you will need to have a patent search performed by a lawyer or professional patent searcher at a cost of $500.00 or more—possibly much more. You know you can't afford to spend that much money on an idea that someone else may well have thought of already. Maybe you should just forget about it.

Well, think again. The fact is you can do your own patent search in your spare time, and with only a reasonable amount of effort. Even better, you can do this without spending more than a few dollars. If it turns out that your idea has never before been addressed in a patent, it may be that its time for a patent has come. And depending on what you do with that patent, you may gain a new amount of independence and ability to fulfill your life goals.

As we explain in Chapter 1, an invention must be judged both novel and unobvious (surprising in light of prior developments) to receive a patent. The novelty of your idea will be judged not only against all previously issued patents, but also against all previous developments in the same field, whether or not they were ever patented. For instance, the grooves in an automobile steering wheel were deemed to be a non-patentable invention because of the traditional use of grooves in sword handles. This rule means that to be absolutely sure that your idea is patentable you will have to go beyond the patent database and examine all written references to similar developments and all real-life items that may embody your idea. But that type of comprehensive search can wait until later.

For now, a search of the U.S. patent database is a good place to start. If someone has thought of your idea before, and deemed it valuable, chances are the idea will show up in one or more patents. Keep in mind, however, that pending patent applications (patent applications that have already been submitted, but for which no patent has yet been issued) are kept confidential for 18 months and cannot be searched until that time has been exceeded. (See Chapter 10 for further discussion on pending patent applications.)

What is the Patent Database?

The U.S. patent database contains all of the patents issued by the United States Patent and Trademark Office (PTO) from the beginning of the country. Individual patents are stored in patent file folders at the PTO in Virginia. Additionally, the PTO has created a computer database of patent images and text.

The traditional method of searching the patent database is to hire a search professional to travel to the U.S. Patent and Trademark Office in Virginia and conduct the search there. While very effective, this process is also very expensive. However, you can save yourself some money by performing a preliminary search yourself. If your search reveals that your idea has already been described in one or more previous patents, you will have saved yourself the expense of hiring a search professional.

You don't have to go to Virginia to perform your preliminary search. Instead, you can use the World Wide Web. The PTO provides an online database where you simply type in words which describe your

invention—called keywords--to search for patents as far back as 1971 that contain those same words. Pre-1971 patents can also be searched on a much more limited basis.

Another great resource for patent searching is a network of special libraries called Patent and Trademark Depository Libraries (PTDL's—see Appendix A for a list). At a PTDL you can perform computer searches of the PTO's electronic database.

As you learn how to search for patents, you also will learn how to think about your ideas in the same way that the patent office would were you to apply for a patent on them. This knowledge will enable you to search for ideas that are not only the same as yours, but similar to yours. This process will allow you to determine not only if your invention is the first, but also whether it is the best. And if it is not, the search may inspire you to refine your idea in ways that will qualify it for a patent.

Key to assessing the patentability of your new idea is understanding what previous developments—known in the trade as prior art—the patent office will consider when deciding whether to issue a patent on your idea. This book will help you to:

- understand how the patent office classifies different types of inventions

- assign your idea to the right class

- compare your idea to other similar ideas in the same class, and

- tentatively conclude whether your idea is new enough to qualify for a patent.

By doing your own preliminary patent search, you will become educated about the true nature of your idea. Strangely enough, many people who come up with new ideas—including full time inventors—often do not fully understand what they have invented. They may dwell on one particular aspect of their invention, and miss a much more valuable general concept that is revealed to them in the course of their patent search.

For example, suppose you want to invent a system to deploy a banner from a hot air balloon. For airplanes, banners simply need to be dragged behind the airplane. The speed of the aircraft, combined with the wake of the plane, will then cause the banner to be unfurled.

However, balloons travel much more slowly than airplanes. If you want to deploy a banner in the horizontal direction, you will need to insert a retractable rod into one side of the banner. You design an air cylinder and rod system, using compressed gas to deploy the rod. Since weight and cost are considerations, you use nitrogen as your compressed gas.

As an after thought, you check the U.S. patent database for similar designs. You find out that no one has patented a retractable banner system for balloons using compressed nitrogen and a rod. Your search reveals that compressed nitrogen has been used to inflate air bags, but not banners. But wait, inflating air bags with compressed nitrogen makes you to realize that the rod itself could be eliminated from your design. Compressed nitrogen alone could be used to inflate an inner chamber in the banner. This will greatly simplify the design. Hold on, why limit yourself to nitrogen when you could use any compressed fluid? You now have a much more general deployment system that can be used in several applications.

Performing patent searches is a great way to get familiar with patent terminology. This will come in handy during all aspects of the patent search as well as the patent application process itself. In particular,

when dealing directly with the patent examiner who is reviewing your application, it helps if you are both speaking the same language.

B. Check Product Submissions

So far we have addressed you as if you are an inventor, whether formal or informal. But this book can also be of great benefit if you are a business owner who, because of the nature of your business, tends to be approached by people who want you to manufacture or distribute their new invention. The outside inventor wants you to invest thousands of dollars in special tooling, and related manufacturing or marketing costs. The idea seems good. It looks like it will enhance your existing product line. But how do you know that another company is not making the same, or a similar product? If another company is manufacturing a similar product, you need to know about this before investing time, money and effort on the submitted idea. This does not necessarily preclude the submission, but gives you a warning flag to seek an expert opinion before proceeding.

Business owners often spend thousands of dollars on professional patent searchers to verify the uniqueness of new product submissions. This cost can add up quickly. As a business owner, you can save yourself considerable amounts of money by performing some of this searching yourself. Additionally, with the cost savings you realize, you will be able to evaluate more new products. This can be an especially valuable benefit if your business has a tight operating budget.

This book can help you "check out" new product ideas. You can also monitor new patents issued for devices in your line of business. By doing so, you can help your company advance with the leading edge of technology. You will also see what patents are owned by your competitors. This will help reduce the chances of having a nasty surprise product turn up on the shelves—a product which does everything that yours does, but at half the cost.

C. Save Time and Money

Performing your own preliminary patent search can save you a lot of money and time. If you want the patent office to grant you a patent on a particular invention, you will have to file what is known as a patent application. It is essential to perform a patent search before filing. Why? Because, filing a patent application, with its associated specification, drawings and fees, is an expensive, time consuming process— often costing up to $10000 or more, if you have it done by a patent attorney. You can, however, do it yourself for far less money with the help of *Patent It Yourself* by David Pressman (Nolo). Either way, before setting out to file a patent application, you will want to be reasonably sure, at the very least, that your idea has not been trumped by a previous patent.

As mentioned, the average cost of a single preliminary patent search performed by a patent search professional is around $500.00. By using the techniques in this book, you will be able to do most, if not all, of this work yourself. If you have lots of ideas and you are trying to select the best one to patent, you can save some really serious money. This is because a professional patent searcher will charge you separately for each invention. For example, if you want four ideas searched, the cost

easily could be $2000. Even if you ultimately decide to use a professional patent searcher, you can perform some of the preliminary searching yourself. This may save you a portion of the search fees and make you a more knowledgeable client.

D. Avoid Reinventing the Wheel

By checking the U.S. patent database first, you can avoid spending a lot of time tweaking your invention, only to find out later that you have reinvented the wheel. For example, suppose that your favorite hobby is amateur astronomy. You love to spend endless hours under the night sky with your telescope. One problem you have is reading the sky charts and comparing them with what you see through the eyepiece of the telescope. You purchased a red light nightlight because the red light does not interfere with your night vision. But you keep losing the nightlight or you have to hold the nightlight and fumble with the chart while switching your vision back and forth between the eyepiece and the chart.

Then it hits you. You will invent a special attachment for the nightlight; an attachment that will allow you to clip it to whatever is handy. Over the next several days you spend hours coming up with several designs; nightlights with clips, nightlights with screws, and nightlights with rubber bands. Finally, you have it. The best solution is a nightlight with a flexible housing that can be wrapped around any convenient nearby structure. You've invented the flexible astronomy nightlight! Wrong, you've reinvented the snake light.

E. How to Use "Patent Searching Made Easy"

ICON KEY

➜ Skip Ahead
📖 More Information

These icons are used throughout this book.

This book is arranged in four parts:

- Part One: The Basics
- Part Two: Internet-Based Patent Searching
- Part Three: PDTL-Based Patent Searching
- Part Four: Where Do I Go from Here?

Part one gives you your basic training. Here, we help you come up with words to describe your invention. These are known as keywords or search words. Once you come up with these words, you can use your computer to search the U.S. patent database for patents that contain these words. In addition to searching for isolated occurrences of your individual search terms, you can also search for combinations of search terms. Often, the use of words in combination will produce much more targeted or specific search results. For your information, the rules of logic that control how we combine keywords are known as Boolean logic. In Chapter 1, we will review Boolean logic in detail, and show how you use it to get the best possible search results. In Chapter 2, we will cover the required hardware, software, and windows skills necessary for doing patent searches on the Internet.

In Part Two, you will perform simple and advanced patent searches using the Internet. You will use different keywords and vary their combinations with Boolean logic. We will also introduce you to the USPTO's classification system. These are the categories that the PTO uses to classify or sort the various types of inventions. Here we will help you discover what category the USPTO will most likely use for your invention. Once we identify these categories, we will show you how to search for other patents within the same category. This will tell you what patents have issued for inventions similar to yours.

Part Two also covers:

- Searching at the European Patent Office (EPO)
- Use a translation service to translate foreign language patents.
- Searching non-patent resources

In Part three we cover the resources available at the nationwide network of Patent and Trademark Depository Libraries (PTDLs). These resources include:

- Using the following printed manuals: the *Index to the U.S. Patent Classification*, *Manual of Classification* and *Classification Definitions*.
- Using the Classification And Search Support Information System (CASSIS) computer system.
- Using the Examiner Assisted Search Tool (EAST) and the Web-based Examiner Search Tool (WEST).

In Part four we will help you assess the results of your search in terms of their effect on the patentability of your invention.

Part 1

The Basics

In this part of the book, we introduce you to the tools and techniques used to perform a basic preliminary patent search. In Chapter 1, we discuss what a patent is and how word-based patent searches work. In Chapter 2, the computer hardware, software and Windows skills that you will need are reviewed. Chapter 2 also introduces us to the resources available at the Patent and Trademark Depository Library (PTDL).

Chapter

1

Introduction to Patents and Patent Searching

A. What is a patent, and what does it do for me?

A patent is a right, granted by the government, to a person or legal entity (partnership or corporation). A patent gives its holder the right to exclude others from making, using or selling the invention "claimed" in the patent deed for twenty years from the date of filing (For patents issued before June 8, 1995, seventeen years from the date the patent was issued by the U.S. Patent and Trademark Office). Once the patent expires, the invention covered by the patent enters the public domain and can be used by anyone. The scope of a U.S. patent is limited to the borders of the United States and its territories.

The right of exclusion given to a patent owner can best be thought of as an offensive legal right. This right of exclusion allows the patent owner to file a lawsuit in federal court against an infringer (anyone who violates the right of exclusion). Because the right of exclusion is not a defensive legal right, the patent owner can't rely on law enforcement agencies to automatically prosecute someone that infringes (copies) his or her patented invention.

Patent Application Process

When you submit your completed patent application and filing fee to the PTO, you will be assigned a filing date. After a six- to 18- month waiting period, a patent examiner will review the application. While it is possible that your application will be allowed as is, this is usually not the case. More often than not, the patent examiner will object to one or more of your claims, or require changes to your patent drawings or specifications. This results in what is known as an "Office Action." The office action is an official communication (letter) from the patent office, outlining the objections to your original patent application. You then have the choice of either modifying the application or convincing the examiner that he/she was in error.

After you successfully respond to the office action the patent examiner will allow your application and you will have to pay an issue fee. After a few more months' delay, your patent will finally issue. The entire process, from initial patent application submission to issued patent, usually takes from 1.5 to three years.

📖 *For more information about how to complete and file a patent application, see* Patent It Yourself, *by David Pressman (Nolo).*

In the sense that a patent gives the patent holder the right to sue anyone who tries to develop, use or manufacture the invention covered by the patent, the patent can be a valuable commodity. It can be sold outright or licensed in exchange for a royalty. Additionally, the patent owner may choose to manufacture and distribute the invention, thereby keeping all the proceeds for him or herself.

📖 *For more information about licensing inventions, see* License Your Invention, *by Richard Stim (Nolo).*

Patents as a Type of Intellectual Property

A patent falls under the larger category of Intellectual Property. Other forms of intellectual property are Trademarks, Trade Secrets, and Copyrights. Depending on the type of invention, one of these other forms of intellectual property may give you greater offensive legal rights. For example, a trademark would be appropriate if your innovation is a new type of symbol, or word associated with a particular product, or a family of products. Examples of popular trademarks are Diet Coke, and Mr. Coffee. A trade secret would generally be described as any information that, by being kept a secret, gives its owner a competitive business advantage. The formula for Kentucky Fried Chicken is one of the best known examples. Copyright law is used to protect the expressive works of authors, computer programmers, movie producers and other artistic creators.

📖 *For more information about trademarks, trade secrets and copyrights, consult the following resources:* Trademark: Legal Care For Your Business & Product Name, *by Kate McGrath and Stephen Elias (Nolo),* Patent, Copyright & Trademark, *by Stephen Elias (Nolo), and* The Copyright Handbook, *by Stephen Fishman (Nolo).*

1. Categories of Patents

There are three main types of patents: utility patents, design patents and plant patents. In this book, we will focus on utility patents because they are more common. Not surprisingly, a utility patent covers the functional aspects of an invention. As an example, assume that the hammer hasn't been invented yet. Ivan Inventor conceives of the hammer as an invention after he accidentally smashes his thumb with a rock he was using to pound a square peg into a round hole. If Ivan applies for a patent and his patent application describes his hammer invention in general enough terms, the patent would cover all variations of the hammer as a utilitarian device. It would cover common household hammers, sledge hammers, rubber hammers and the like. Perhaps even hydraulic hammers could be covered.

A design patent only covers the appearance of an invention. In our example, Ivan might apply for a design patent for a hammer with a horsehead etched into the shaft of the hammer. Removal of the horsehead would not affect the utility or functioning of the hammer. Design patents are easy to work around. A competitor could design a hammer with a slightly different horsehead, (longer mane or bigger eyes) and the new hammer design most likely would not infringe on the original design patent.

Plant patents are for new types of plants. Because plant patents are uncommon we don't cover them in this book.

2. Patent Eligibility Requirements

In order to get a utility patent (as opposed to a design patent), your patent application has to satisfy four legal criterion. (Novelty, unobviousness and other patent requirements are discussed in greater detail in Chapter 10.)

1. Your invention has to fit into an established Statutory Class.
2. Your invention must have some Utility. In other words, it has to be useful.
3. Your invention must have some Novelty. It must have some physical difference from any similar inventions in the past.
4. Your invention must be Unobvious to someone who is skilled in the appropriate field.

In order to fit within an established Statutory Class (the first legal criterion), your invention must be either a Process, a Machine, an Article of Manufacture, a Composition of Matter or a New Use invention.

- A Process is just the performance of a series of operations on something.

- A Machine is a device consisting of a series of fixed or moving parts that direct mechanical energy towards a specific task.

- An Article of Manufacture can be made by hand or machine. As opposed to machines, Articles of Manufacture are inventions that are relatively simple, with few or no moving parts.

- A Composition of Matter is a unique arrangement of items. Chemical compositions such as glue and plastics are good examples of compositions of matter.

- A New Use process is simply a new way of using an invention that fits in one of the first four statutory classes.

The second criterion your patent application has to satisfy is that it must be useful. Fortunately, any new use will satisfy this requirement. In general if your invention is operable (if it functions), it will satisfy this requirement.

The next requirement is Novelty. To get a patent, your invention must be somehow different from all previous inventions documented in the prior art. Generally, there are three types of difference categories.

1. Physical differences between your invention and previous inventions.
2. New combinations made by using previous aspects of two or more different inventions.
3. A new use of a previous invention.

As mentioned, your invention will also have to be deemed unobvious. This is the toughest of the patent requirements. Essentially, what it means is that your new concept must be a significant step forward in the field of the invention. In other words, if a skilled worker who is thoroughly familiar with developments in the area of your invention would consider the idea obvious, you would fail this test.

3. The Patent Document

In one sense a patent is an abstract notion. The PTO issues a patent. The patent gives you certain affirmative rights. The patent expires in 20 years. You can sell or license your patent. In all these uses, the term patent is an abstraction. In reality, the terms of a patent are spelled out in a document called a patent deed that is produced by the PTO. More commonly, the patent document is simply referred to as a patent or patent reference. The patent database consists of hardcopy, microfiche or electronic copies of patent documents.

Every utility patent document, which we'll simply refer to as a patent from this point on, has several identifiable fields or sections. Understanding the different parts of the patent will be especially important when we cover computer searching. This is because we will conduct our search in

TABLE OF PATENT SECTIONS

Patent Section	Description
Title	Patent title.
Inventor information	Inventor's name and address.
Patent number	The number assigned to the issued patent.
Patent filing date	The date that the patent application was filed with the PTO.
Patent issue date	The date that the patent was issued by the PTO.
Classification	Class and subclass information. These are the categories that the PTO uses to classify or sort the various types of inventions.
Referenced patents	The patent numbers of previous patents referred to in the patent application, along with their classes and subclasses.
Abstract	Usually one concise paragraph that summarizes the invention in plain English. Appears on the front page of the issued patent. This is the most frequently referenced section of the patent.
Drawings	Drawings of the invention from different perspectives.
Background of the invention	Discussion of any previous inventions that were related to this invention. This is known as "prior art".
Summary of the invention	A discussion of the invention that captures its essential functions and features.
Brief description of drawings	A one-sentence description of each patent drawing figure.
Detailed description of the preferred version of the invention	An in-depth discussion of the various aspects of the invention. Painstaking references to the patent drawings are made.
Claims	This section defines the legal scope of the patent (like a deed describes the boundaries of real estate).

certain sub-sections of the patent, and it helps to know what sort of information to expect to find there.

Above is a table showing the typical sections that appear in a patent, along with a brief description of what is in each one. Our table introduces us to several terms commonly used in the patent world. "Class" and "subclass" refer to the complex system used by the PTO to categorize each and every patent that it issues. Conceptually, the system is similar to an alphabetical library index file. For example, to search a library for a book about baseball, one would first go to the subject card index. In the file drawer for subjects beginning with the letter S, you would most likely find a Sports section. Under the sports section, you would go to the subsection for Baseball. There you would find the titles of several books related to baseball. The PTO currently has over 100,000 classes and subclasses.

An "abstract" is simply a summary of the most important features of the invention covered by the patent. The abstract appears on the front page of the issued patent. Patent searchers consult the abstract to get a quick overview of the invention. This in turn helps them decide whether it is worthwhile to review the entire patent. The abstract is the searcher's way to separate the wheat from the chaff. A typical abstract is shown below. This is from patent # 5,712,618, an automatic turn signaling device for vehicles.

no. 1,466,559 - Exercising Device

ABSTRACT

An automatic signaling device for a vehicle which automatically initiates a method and apparatus for an automatic signaling device warning signal to pedestrians and to other vehicles in connection with lane changes and upon turns. The present invention is activated and deactivated automatically providing significant safety advantages for all of those using the roads and highways.

15 Claims, 2 Drawing Figures

The "background of the invention" is a discussion of previous inventions that are related in some way to the current invention. These inventions are known as the prior art of the current invention. These previous inventions may embody some of the same or similar elements as the current invention. For example, sprinkler systems and fireproof blankets are two vastly different products. However, they are both related by the fact that they are fire suppressant devices. So, if you invented a modern-day fire suppression device (for instance one using nanotechnology —tiny microscopic machines—to deprive the fire of oxygen), both sprinkler systems and fireproof blankets would be considered prior art related to your invention.

The first two paragraphs from the background section of patent number 5,712,618 are shown above. The first paragraph is a general summary of the background of the invention. The next paragraph begins the discussion of the advantages of the current invention over previously patented inventions.

BACKGROUND OF THE INVENTION

The invention disclosed herein relates to preferred methods and apparatuses for an automatic signaling device which automatically activates a warning signal. The following patents form a background for the instant invention. None of the cited publications is believed to detract from the patentability of the claimed invention.

U.S. Pat. No. 3,771,096 issued to Walter on Nov. 6, 1973, discloses a lane changing signaling device for vehicles employing a rotary electrical connector joined to the steering wheel. The principal disadvantage of the device is that it fails to measure the angle of rotation of the steering wheel.

Prior art is not limited to inventions patented in the U.S. Patents issued in other countries are considered valid prior art, and, if you apply for a patent, will be compared against your invention. Also, any other published information, from any corner of the globe, can prevent a patent from being granted. Even unpublished works, such as a Masters thesis, can be considered valid prior art. In Chapter 10 we explain how to evaluate your invention in light of the relevant prior art.

The "detailed description of the preferred version of the invention" (*embodiment* in patent terms) is a detailed description of an actual, "nuts and bolts" version of the current invention. It is essentially the inventor's best-guess (preferred embodiment) description of the product, at the time the patent application is written. By reading the detailed description, a person who is familiar with similar products should be able to build and operate the current invention. It is important to note that the legal scope of the patent is not defined (the language of patents calls it "limited") by the details of the description of the preferred embodiment. Rather, the scope of the patent is determined by the "claims" (see below).

The first paragraph of the detailed description of the preferred embodiment for patent number 5,462,805; a fire safety glass panel, is shown below. Reading through the description we see that specific numbered elements of figure number 1 (from patent 5,462,805) are referenced. This figure is shown as figure 1 below. Here we have a glass plate (element 10), another glass plate (element 11), an intermediate resin layer (element 12), and first and second adhesive layers (elements 13 and 14). By following

DESCRIPTION OF THE PREFERRED EMBODIMENT

Referring to **FIG. 1**, a fire-protection and safety glass panel according to a preferred embodiment of this invention comprises a first glass plate **10**, a second glass plate **11** opposite to the first glass plate, and an intermediate resin layer between the first and second glass plates **10** and **11**. At least one of the first and the second glass plates **10** and **11** is a heat-resistant glass plate. The intermediate resin layer comprises a polyethylene terephthalate film (namely, a PET film) **12** and first and second adhesive agent layers **13** and **14** and has a thickness which is not greater than 200 um. The first adhesive agent layer **13** adheres the PET film **12** to the first glass plate **10**. The second adhesive agent layer **14** adheres the

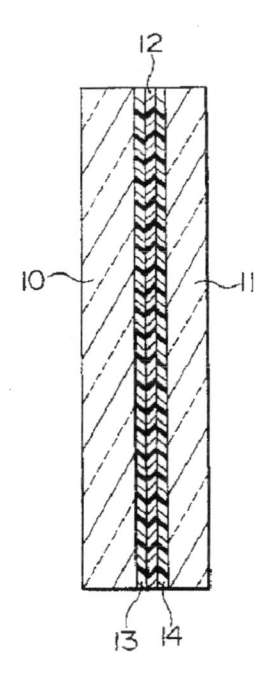

Figure 1

susceptible to being ruled invalid if the patent holder ever finds it necessary to bring an infringement case.

The first claim from the fire safety glass patent (5,462,805) is shown below. While calling out the same elements of the invention as described in the preferred embodiment, the specific element references have been omitted. This is because the claim is meant to be general enough to include different designs based upon the same invention concept.

Also, note that here the glass plates are referred to as "low-expansion crystallized glass." This is broad enough to include many types of glass that do not readily expand when exposed to heat. If a specific type of low-expansion glass were claimed,

along with the detailed description, and matching the numbered elements of the description with the labeled elements of the drawing, a person familiar with fire safety glass would be able to construct this invention.

The "claims" of the patent are a series of tersely worded statements that precisely describe and define the underlying invention. As we suggest in the chart, patent claims operate in much the same way as do real estate deeds—they precisely delimit the scope of the patent in the same way as the real estate deed describes the precise location of the property.

From the patent applicant's viewpoint, the claims should be as broad as possible, thus covering many possible versions of the same basic invention. Broad claims make it difficult for someone to defeat the patent by making a minor change to the invention. On the flip side, if patent claims are too broad, there is always the possibility of someone finding a previous invention (prior art reference) that falls within the patent's scope. This could make the patent

CLAIMS

What is claimed is:
1. A fire-protection and safety glass panel comprising a first glass plate, a second glass plate opposite to said first glass plate, and an intermediate resin layer between said first and said second glass plates, at least one of said first and said second glass plates being a low-expansion crystallized glass plate of a low-expansion crystallized glass, wherein said intermediate resin layer comprises a polyethylene terephthalate film, a first adhesive agent layer for adhering said polyethylene terephthalate film to said first glass plate, and a second adhesive agent layer for adhering said polyethylene terephthalate film to said second glass plate, said intermediate resin layer having a thickness which is not greater than 200 um.

then the patent could be "worked around" by simply claiming a different type of low-expansion glass.

B. Understanding Patent Databases

In order to get the most benefit from a word-based computer search, it is useful to first understand how searchable databases are put together. Creating a computer database is basically a two step process. First, the information has to be entered into the computer. Then, the information has to be processed by a special kind of computer program so that the information can be easily retrieved in a meaningful form.

There are generally two ways to get information into a computer (not including voice recognition hardware and software, which is still not commonly used). Someone can physically type the data in at the keyboard, or a person can make use of a device called a scanner. A scanner is similar to the everyday copy machine. A page is placed on a surface and a machine records an image of what's on the page. However, when a scanner is connected to a computer, it is possible to capture an image of a document and store that image on the hard disk of the computer.

When a document is scanned into a computer, it may take one of two forms:

- an image, or
- text that has been extracted from the scanned document by software known as OCR (Optical Character Recognition).

For the purpose of searching by computer, there is a big difference between an image of a document that hasn't been subjected to OCR software and the text that an OCR scan produces. If, for example, a patent is scanned into a computerized database without OCR treatment, the contents of the image can't be searched; after all, it's just a picture. The computer has no way of knowing what the picture contains. You can pull up the patent on your computer screen the same as any other graphical image, but you can't search for the patent according to the words contained in it. However, if the text in the patent document is read by an OCR program before it makes its way into the database, the database will be able to index the text and pull up the patent document according to the words contained in a keyword search.

The database that gets created as a result of OCR processing (or of text that is manually entered or already in computer-readable form) is essentially a huge lookup table. The program that builds this table searches through all the entered text and extracts all the meaningful words. Then, these words, along with a link to the original document they were found in, are placed into the lookup table.

When you use a computer program to perform a word-based search, the program matches the search words you type in with words stored in its lookup table. The search words that you enter are called "keywords" and the search process is called a keyword search. If the computer finds a match, the program will report back to you the document in which the word was found and, in some cases, the location of the word within the document.

The lookup table ("database" in computer talk) is similar to indexes found in the back of many books. In book indexes, words are listed alphabetically, along with a comma-separated list of each page in the book where the word was used.

C. Understanding Keyword Searching

When you use a computer program to search for patents, you often must search for them by entering words into a "query" box and asking the search program to match your words with words stored in its database.

As you might expect, performing keyword searches is a skill with a learning curve. Sure, anyone can put one or two words into a box and pull up all the patents with those words. No skill there. But the overall number of patents you pull up is likely to be huge and the number of the patents that are relevant to your search is likely to be low. To pull up a manageable number of patents and to assure that most of them will have some relevance to your own invention, you will need to know at least some of the basic techniques for choosing your search terms and combining them into meaningful search queries.

1. The Role of Wildcards in Keyword Searching

One powerful tool that is often used during keyword searching is called the wildcard. A wildcard is a special character inserted into your keyword. This character tells the computer search program to do something special with the keyword within which it's used. The two most often used wildcard symbols are the dollar sign '$', and the question mark '?'.

The dollar sign wildcard is used at the end of a word root to take the place of any number of additional letters that may come after that root. For example, assume you

have invented a new type of dance shoe. The shoe can be used for ballroom, ballet and tap dancing. In addition to the keywords "ballroom," "ballet" and "tap," you will certainly want to search for the word "dance." But there are several variations of the word "dance," such as, "dancing," "dancer," "danced," and even "danceable." By using "danc$" as your keyword, the dollar sign replaces any other possible characters that would follow the four letters, "danc."

Figure 2, below, contains the search results from searching the titles of U.S. patents issued in the years 1997-1998 for the word "dance." The patent titles that have the word "dance" in them are listed and numbered. As you can see, there are four patents that have the word "dance" in the title. The first title relates to a dance practice slipper, the second title concerns the sole of a dance shoe, the third title relates to a type of dance and the fourth title relates to a portable dance floor.

Refine Search

ISD/1/1/1997->12/31/1998 and ttl/dance

PAT. NO.	Title
1 D388,592	**T** Dance practice slipper
2 5,682,685	**T** Dance shoe sole
3 PP9,938	**T** Peach tree "Snow Dance"
4 5,634,309	**T** Portable dance floor

Figure 2 (Source: USPTO Website)

Figure 3, below, contains the search results from searching the titles of U.S. patents issued in the years 1997-1998 for the word "danc$." As you can see, we now have nine patents listed. The first patent listed (patent number 5,827,107) contains the word "dancing" as opposed to "dance."

Refine Search	ISD/1/1/1997->12/31/1998 and ttl/danc$

PAT. NO.   Title

1 <u>5,827,107</u> **T** <u>Spinning dancing top</u>

2 <u>D388,592</u> **T** <u>Dance practice slipper</u>

3 <u>5,682,685</u> **T** <u>Dance shoe sole</u>

4 <u>5,669,117</u> **T** <u>Buckle for line dancing</u>

5 <u>D382,902</u> **T** <u>Unit for teaching dancing</u>

6 <u>5,659,229</u> **T** <u>Controlling web tension by actively controlling velocity of dancer roll</u>

7 <u>PP9,938</u>   **T** <u>Peach tree "Snow Dance"</u>

8 <u>5,634,309</u> **T** <u>Portable dance floor</u>

9 <u>5,602,747</u> **T** <u>Controlling web tension by actively controlling velocity of dancer roll</u>

Figure 3 (Source: USPTO Website)

The first four letters (danc) are the same as in the word "dance," but the wildcard ($) was used for the letters "ing." The next two titles are the same ones that we obtained before. However, title numbers 4 and 5 also contain the word "dancing" as opposed to "dance." Similarly, title numbers 6 and 9, contain the word "dancer," as opposed to "dance." Here, the wildcard ($) was used for the letters "er."

The question mark (?) wildcard can be used to replace any single character in a word. Continuing with our dancing example, the words "foot" or "feet" could be searched by using "f??t" as our keyword. Obviously, you would not want to use the keyword "f$", as this would return every word that started with the letter "f." By using "f??t," every four-letter word that starts with "f" and ends with "t" would be searched for by the computer. For example, along with the words "feet" and "foot", the words "flat" and "fast" would also be reported to you in the search results.

In Figure 4 below, we show the search results obtained from searching the titles of U.S. patents issued on 12/9/1997 for the word "f??t." The first two patents listed (Pat. Nos. 5696609 and 5696529), contain the word "flat" in the title. The next two patents listed (Pat. Nos. 5696435 and 5695530) contain the word "fast" in the title. The fifth and sixth patents listed (Pat. Nos. 5695527 and 5695526), contain the word 'foot' in the title. The seventh, eighth, ninth and tenth patents listed (Pat. Nos. 5695,360, 5695,359, 5,694,834 and 5695792), contain the word "flat" in the title. Finally, the eleventh patent listed (Design Pat. No. D387,428), contains the word "foot" in the title.

Refine Search | ISD/12/9/1997->12/9/1997 and ttl/f??t

PAT. NO.   Title

1 5,696,609 **T** Illumination system for a flat-bed scanning system

2 5,696,529 **T** Flat panel monitor combining direct view with overhead projection capability

3 5,696,435 **T** Fast battery charger for a device having a varying electrical load during recharging

4 5,695,530 **T** Method for making high charging efficiency and fast oxygen recombination rechargeable hydride batteries

5 5,695,527 **T** Coil prosthetic foot

6 5,695,526 **T** One-piece mechanically differentiated prosthetic foot and associated ankle joint with syme modification

7 5,695,360 **T** Zero insertion force electrical connector for flat cable

8 5,695,359 **T** Zero insertion force electrical connector for flat cable

9 5,694,834 **T** Device for forming in series flat objects of adjustable shape and thickness by deposition of a relatively fluid substance on a support

10 5,694,792 **T** Needle selection device of flat knitting machine

11 D387,428 **T** Transparent x-ray film cassette holder for x-ray of a foot and ankle

Figure 4 (Source: USPTO Website)

2. The Role of Boolean Logic in Keyword Patent Searching

A search technique known as Boolean logic can be used to combine individual keywords into powerful searches. Boolean logic uses a total of four words (called "logical operators") to define the search: AND, OR, XOR, and ANDNOT. The AND operator is by far the most useful. A graphical representation known as a Venn diagram will help you to understand how these operators work.

In Figure 5 below, we have a circle that has been shaded. The area inside the circle represents all of the patents that contain the keyword represented by the letter A. The area outside the circle represents all the other patents that do not contain the keyword represented by A. In other words, if we were to search a database of patents for all the occurrences of the keyword A, our search results would be contained in the shaded circle above.

In Figure 6, below, we have two keywords represented by the circles A and B. Searching for individual occurrences of the keywords A or B would result in a lot of search results. It would take a long time to review these results and most of them would be irrelevant.

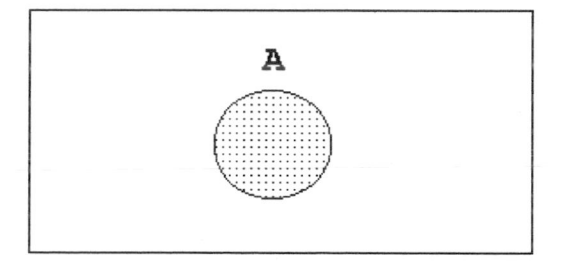

Figure 5

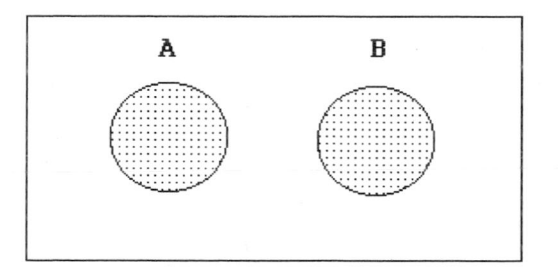

Figure 6

For example, let's suppose we have an invention idea for a new type of telephone cable. A search for the keyword telephone would return numerous references to different types of telephones. Similarly, a keyword search for the word cable would return patents related to cable television, bridge support cables, cable cars, and so on. What we need is a way to search for both the keywords telephone and cable within the same patent. This is where Boolean operators come into the picture.

3. The AND Boolean Operator

In Figure 7 below, we have used the Boolean operator AND to combine the keywords A and B. The shaded area where the circles overlap represents the search results that contain both keywords A and B. As you can see, the AND operator is a great way to narrow the scope of the search.

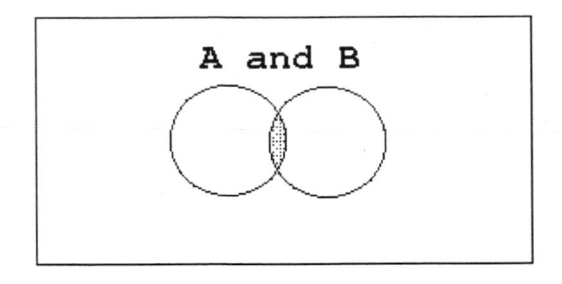

Figure 7

When a match is found between a keyword (or a combination of keywords) and a patent, the result is called a "Hit." When patent searches are conducted, the number of hits, or occurrences, of a keyword match is usually reported to the user. By using the AND operator, the user reduces the quantity of hits that need to be reviewed.

For example, let's suppose that you have invented a new type of steam engine. A steam engine is a machine for converting the

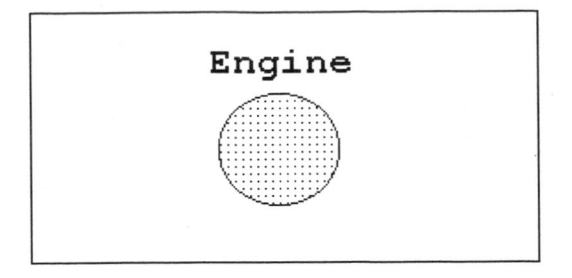

Figure 8

heat energy in steam into mechanical energy by means of a piston moving in a cylinder.

The search results using the keyword Engine are shown in Figure 8 above. The shaded circle represents all of the patents that contain the word Engine. This could be quite an extensive list. For example, all the various types of internal combustion engines would be included in this list. A steam-powered vehicle is an external combustion device; the steam is usually obtained from an external boiler. However, if we only searched for the word Engine, we would have to review search results that contained references to gasoline-powered engines for cars, trucks, trains and all other engine-powered devices.

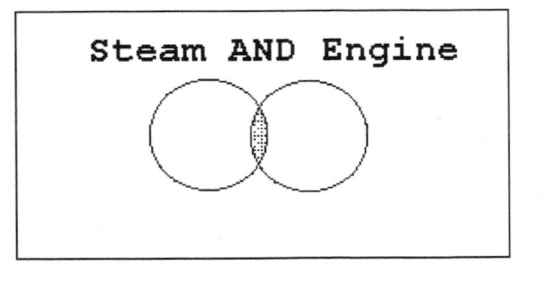

Figure 9

Figure 9 above, shows the search result obtained when using the Boolean AND operator to combine the keywords Steam and Engine. The resulting number of hits is represented by the small shaded area in the diagram, where the two circles overlap. We can see at once why AND is the most often